ERICA R. DIUGUID

THE TRUE
LIFETIME
COMMITMENT

Scripture quotations marked (NIV) are taken from the Holy Bible, New International Version®, NIV®. Copyright © 1973, 1978, 1984, 2011 by Biblica, Inc.™ Used by permission of Zondervan. All rights reserved worldwide. www.zondervan.com The "NIV" and "New International Version" are trademarks registered in the United States Patent and Trademark Office by Biblica, Inc.™

"Scripture quotations marked (ESV) are from The ESV® Bible (The Holy Bible, English Standard Version®), copyright © 2001 by Crossway, a publishing ministry of Good News Publishers. Used by permission. All rights reserved."

Scripture taken from the New Century Version®. Copyright © 2005 by Thomas Nelson. Used by permission. All rights reserved.

Scripture quotations marked (NLT) are taken from the Holy Bible, New Living Translation, copyright ©1996, 2004, 2015 by Tyndale House Foundation. Used by permission of Tyndale House Publishers, Inc., Carol Stream, Illinois 60188. All rights reserved.

Scripture quotations taken from the New American Standard Bible® (NASB), Copyright © 1960, 1962, 1963, 1968, 1971, 1972, 1973, 1975, 1977, 1995 by The Lockman Foundation Used by permission. www.Lockman.org"

Scripture taken from the New King James Version®. Copyright © 1982 by Thomas Nelson. Used by permission. All rights reserved.

"Scripture quotations taken from the Amplified® Bible (AMP), Copyright © 2015 by The Lockman Foundation
Used by permission. www.Lockman.org"

The Holy Bible, Berean Study Bible, BSB. Copyright ©2016, 2018 by Bible Hub. Used by Permission. All Rights Reserved Worldwide.

Scripture quoted by permission. Quotations designated (NET) are from the NET Bible® copyright ©1996-2016 by Biblical Studies Press, L.L.C. http://netbible.com
All rights reserved.

Scripture quotations marked (NIrV) are taken from the Holy Bible, New International Reader's Version®, NIrV® Copyright © 1995, 1996, 1998, 2014 by Biblica, Inc.™ Used by permission of Zondervan. All rights reserved worldwide. www.zondervan.com The "NIrV" and "New International

Reader's Version" are trademarks registered in the United States Patent and Trademark Office by Biblica, Inc.™

Copyright © 2019 by Erica R. Bluford

All rights reserved. No part of this book may be reproduced or used in any manner without written permission of the publisher except for the use of quotations in a book review. For more information, address: thetruelifetimecommitment@gmail.com

FIRST EDITION

ISBN 978-0-5785-0047-8 (paperback)

Cover Design by Bradley Burton, Burton Designs

Views, thoughts, and opinions expressed herein belong solely to the author and not necessarily to any organization, committee, other group, or individual. The author is a Christian author and has formed her thoughts through her own personal research, personal experiences, and under the guidance of the Holy Spirit. You are encouraged to be a discerning reader.

While the author has made every effort to provide accurate citations and information at the time of publication, she assumes no responsibility for errors, oversights, or for changes that occur after publication. She denies any liability to any party for any loss, damage, or disruption caused by errors or omissions whether such errors or omissions result from negligence, accident, or any other cause.

Contents

Acknowledgements i
Introduction iii
Devotions
    Day 1: You Are Not Crazy 1
    Day 2: The Standard 3
    Day 3: Be Made New 5
    Day 4: A New Heart 7
    Day 5: Find Your Identity 9
    Day 6: Why We Need A Devotional 11
    Day 7: Rest In The Presence Of God 13
    Day 8: A Good Thing, Or A God Thing? 15
    Day 9: Putting God First 17
    Day 10: Love Your Neighbor 19
    Day 11: Don't Deceive Your Brother 21
    Day 12: Be Gentle With Your Neighbor 23
    Day 13: Love Yourself 25
    Day 14: Rest In The Presence Of God 27
    Day 15: Comfortable Christianity 29
    Day 16: Pleasing God vs. Pleasing Man 31
    Day 17: Am I Still A Christian If…? 33
    Day 18: The Devil Made Me Do It 35
    Day 19: Dust Yourself Off And Try Again 37
    Day 20: Dealing With Consequences 39
    Day 21: Rest In The Presence Of God 42
    Day 22: Fruit of the Spirit vs. Fruit of the Flesh 44
    Day 23: Why Me? 45
    Day 24: Confidently Christian 46
    Day 25: Close The Door 48
    Day 26: Do Your Research 50
    Day 27: Join The Team 52
    Day 28: Rest In The Presence Of God 54
    Day 29: An Everyday Choice 56
    Day 30: Pressing Forward 58
Conclusion 60

Acknowledgements

First, to my parents, Eric and Keisha Bluford: thank you for praying for me; for teaching me the way I should go; for allowing me to make mistakes and praying that I would return; for being excellent role models; for loving and supporting me; for showing me that I don't have to be bored or boring to be a Christian; and for just being real. I am grateful for you both, and I'm so happy that God entrusted me to you!

To my sisters, Erice and Erin; thank you for motivating me to be a good role model; for supporting me, even when what I am doing requires you to sacrifice your time, our parents, or whatever you have going on; and for making me laugh, especially at myself.

To my Pastor, Keisha Bluford and my church family at Grace Outreach Ministry: thank you for allowing me to exercise my gifts; for being receptive whenever I present a new idea; and for encouraging me to walk in whatever God calls me to do. Your kindness has been essential in my feeling comfortable writing this set of devotions.

To Nora Richmond, one of my best friends and trusted accountability partners: you have been with me through every major event in my life. I am so thankful for your support and your honesty.

Lastly, thank you Jerry and Tanisha Flowers of Redefined TV and Jamal and Natasha Miller of Married and Young: I participated in the "God Sent vs. Counterfeit" webinar in 2017 thinking I'd learn how to find a spouse. I was pleasantly surprised to be pushed closer to God in a way that had nothing to do with marriage; a necessary push toward spiritual growth and obedience.

Your ministries have been crucial to my journey, and I thank you all for being beacons of wisdom and light for my generation.

Introduction

In 2014 I pledged a sorority – the probate or "coming out" was legendary. There was a sea of smiling faces: peers, my mother and her line sisters, friends, and family. A sea of smiling faces…except for one. My Nanner (paternal grandmother) sat in the front row "priority" seating with a frown on her face. "I don't like this at all," she said, "this is demonic." Rather than listening to her, we were upset that she'd taken up quality seating. After all, more supportive people would have loved to sit there. Ignoring the obvious concerns of my Nanner, I basked in the fact that I was officially Greek. I'd joined for the networking and community programing but was just as engulfed in the partying and sexual sin that came with being an active undergraduate member of Greek life. I was raised in the church so I figured that no matter what I was doing, my salvation was still secure. Sure, there were some people along the way who echoed my Nanner's sentiments on Greek life, but I didn't listen. I went on to become President of the undergraduate chapter at my school and upon graduation joined the alumnae chapter. My connection to the sorority remained constant and I was proud of it.

My mother began seminary in 2015 and one of her classmates told her that Greek life and Christianity were incongruent. I researched what her colleague said but, admittedly, focused on information that affirmed my membership. Shortly thereafter, my mother and I started having dreams regarding our membership in the sorority. Then, a few weeks after I was elected Vice President of the alumnae chapter, I heard the voice of the Lord speaking to me regarding my commitment to sorority life. God said, "Erica, what are you doing? It is time for you to leave. Why aren't you listening to me?" This was the first time I'd heard the voice of the Lord that clearly. I needed no other confirmation. I heard from God myself! My next steps were sort of a blur. I did unbiased research. I compared the sorority's ritual to the Bible. I talked to my line sisters. I consulted with more seasoned members – none of them had answers. I was told about people who remained in Greek organizations (without paying dues or wearing letters) because it offered them better opportunities to spread the gospel to other members from the inside. However, if they renounced Greek life, they would lose access. I could not justify taking that route. Nothing could convince me to stay. How could I? God had spoken to me directly. Over the next few weeks I resigned as Vice President of the alumnae chapter, explained my decision to my line sisters and a few other Greek friends, and began the formal process of renouncing my membership.

Renouncing my membership in Greek life was relatively easy. I remember getting my official letter in August of 2016 – I'd been removed from the organization and could never reapply. I breathed a sigh of relief. I was content in my decision to renounce. However, as founder's days, anniversaries, and probates passed by, and as my Greek friends' birthdays came, I struggled to find balance between my former life and the life I was choosing to lead now. I began to realize that I was lost and a little empty. When I was thinking about renouncing, there was no end to the videos and articles I could review that helped convince me to leave the sorority. Now that I was out, things were silent and the resources for what to do next were non-existent. I was in desperate need of a renewed mind and a transformed heart. I am lucky to have a praying mother taking the exit journey with me; but so many people don't have that. This set of devotions is what I think I needed as I dealt with the mixed emotions of trying to be obedient to God while still missing my former life. This is not an attempt to bash Greek life. Although I may hint to my experiences, I won't go into much detail, and I won't be revealing any Greek secrets. If that's what you are looking for, you'll be disappointed. I hope these devotions will help you get closer to God so that you can gain clarity as well as find healing. Hopefully, you will find wholeness. I pray that your mind and spirit will be renewed. May strongholds be demolished, and may your heart be cleansed.

DEVOTIONS

DAY 1
You Are Not Crazy

> *"This is what we speak, not in words taught us by human wisdom but in words taught by the Spirit, explaining spiritual realities with Spirit taught words. The person without the Spirit does not accept the things that come from the Spirit of God but considers them foolishness, and cannot understand them because they are discerned only through the Spirit."* – 1 Corinthians 2:13-14 (NIV)

> *"And do not be conformed to this world, but be transformed by the renewing of your mind, that you may prove what is that good and acceptable and perfect will of God."* – Romans 12:2 (NKJV)

> *"For the flesh desires what is contrary to the Spirit, and the Spirit what is contrary to the flesh. They are in conflict with each other, so that you are not to do whatever you want."*
> – Galatians 5:17 (NIV)

DEVOTION

I applaud you for being willing to complete the first day of these devotions! I want to encourage you and to let you know that you are not crazy. I cannot count the number of times I heard, "God didn't tell you that" or "I can't really say what God spoke to you," or "Well, I didn't hear that," when I first decided to renounce Greek life. At first, I would get offended and even discouraged by these comments. If not for me hearing the voice of God for myself, there is a better chance I would have been swayed by these comments. However, Scripture reminds us that we are taught spiritual realities through the Holy Spirit, not the comments of others. Despite what many believe, none of us are always operating in the Spirit. We have to check ourselves often. When we don't seek God; when we don't surrender ourselves to God's will; spiritual realities will be considered foolish to us. Foolish because our flesh does not desire or comprehend the same things as the Spirit. When Jesus Christ – a radical Jew who openly taught against centuries of religious tradition came – I am sure that people called him more than foolish. However, Jesus Christ didn't allow name-calling, or even the torment of dying on the cross, to deter him from fulfilling his assignment from God. Jesus was in tune with the Spirit and knew to follow what God told him, no matter what people thought, said, or did. We should strive to do the same. At the end of the day, I would much rather dwell in the foolishness of God than to operate in my own "wisdom." My sister or brother, I tell you today that you are not crazy! Just because the Holy Spirit has not revealed the same thing to your naysayers does not mean that what you heard from God or what you feel is invalid. Your reservations are real. Listen and don't let others deter you. What has been revealed to you has been revealed to other believers. Press forward in the truth that God has given you!

PRAYER

Holy Spirit, I thank you for granting me spiritual wisdom and for revealing to me the mysteries of this world. I pray that I would become more comfortable with being set apart. I pray that I would not be offended when others call me foolish or crazy, but that I would be more like Jesus who was un-phased by name- calling. I desire to be fully convinced in the truth that you have revealed to me and determined to do exactly what you have called me to do. I trust you God. I recognize you as the All-Knowing God. I believe in your word. I submit to your will. In the name of Jesus I pray. Amen.

DAY 2
The Standard

> *"But just as he who called you is holy, so be holy in all you do; for it is written: "Be holy, because I am holy." – 1 Peter 1:15 (NIV)*

> *"But if anyone obeys his word, love for God is truly made complete in them. This is how we know we are in him: Whoever claims to live in him must live as Jesus did." – 1 John 2:5-6 (NIV)*

> *"There is a way that appears to be right, but in the end it leads to death." – Proverbs 14:12 (NIV)*

DEVOTION

On numerous occasions I have questioned myself, and I have certainly been questioned by others because I know very spiritual people who are members of fraternities, sororities, or other secret societies. When these types of questions are asked, it is important to remember that spiritual people, your family, and even your Pastor are not the standard for what is right. God is our standard. When considering whether or not we should do something, we should always seek guidance from God and yield to the example of Jesus Christ. We are all human and humans are subject to error. There are countless times in history when people thought they were doing the right thing, for centuries even, only to later realize that they were completely wrong. Yes, there are Pastors in Greek organizations. Many Greek organizations even have Chaplains assigned to leading them spiritually. That still does not mean that being in the organization is okay. When determining whether something is right, compare your actions to those of Jesus Christ. Truly look and see if the principles of the organization align with the commands of God. Don't let your Pastor, or even me, convince you that something is right, or wrong, because they are doing it. Make the comparison for yourself and make sure you are comparing to the right standard – God.

PRAYER

Dear Lord, I pray that you would open my eyes and my ears that I may see you and that I may hear your voice. I pray that you would increase my desire to seek you for myself. I desire to know you fully so I will be able to know when I have stepped out of your will. Lord, let me not look to the left or to the right for the example of righteousness; but allow me to look straight ahead towards you: the perfect example of what is good. Help me to be more and more like Jesus every day. In the name of Jesus I pray. Amen.

NOTES

DAY 3
Be Made New

"Therefore, if anyone is in Christ, the new creation has come: The old has gone, the new is here!" – 2 Corinthians 5:17 (NIV)

"If we confess our sins, he is faithful and just and will forgive us our sins and purify us from all unrighteousness." – 1 John 1:9 (NIV)

"You were taught, with regard to your former way of life, to put off your old self, which is being corrupted by its deceitful desires; to be made new in the attitude of your minds; and to put on the new self, created to be like God in true righteousness and holiness"
– Ephesians 4:22-24 (NIV)

"We were buried therefore with him by baptism into death, in order that, just as Christ was raised from the dead by the glory of the Father, we too might walk in newness of life."
– Romans 6:4 (ESV)

DEVOTION

When I first pledged, I received a "new name," a "new life," and I committed to be a member for a lifetime. When God called me out of the sorority, many told me that I would always be a member but that is simply not true. To say that I could not renounce my membership would be saying that my God is not powerful enough to sever the ties of the sorority and provide me with a new life. Scriptures assure me that God has the ability to forgive us of our sins, cleanse us, and make us new. God is the only one who has the ability to give us a new life. In God we may have a fresh start. We do not have to remain shackled to our past. We do not have to be the person people always assumed we would be. In Christ we are new creatures and this applies to any sin we may have committed. Do not believe the lies of the enemy. Take off your old self and walk in the newness of life.

PRAYER

Dear Lord, today I recognize that you are the one who makes all things new. I pray now that you would forgive me of my sins and cleanse me from all unrighteousness. Help me to forgive myself so that I may embrace that I am a new creature and so that I may truly walk in the newness of life. Renew my heart and renew my mind, Lord. Teach me how to live a new life that is totally committed to you. In the name of Jesus I pray. Amen.

NOTES

DAY 4
A New Heart

> *"You brood of vipers, can you who are evil say anything good? For the mouth speaks what the heart is full of. A good man brings good things out of the good stored up in him, and an evil man brings evil things out of the evil stored up in him."*
> *– Matthew 12:34-35 (NIV)*

> *"Above all else, guard your heart, for everything you do flows from it." – Proverbs 4:23 (NIV)*

DEVOTION

Your heart is one of the most important organs in your body. In the physical sense, the heart pumps blood throughout the body while carrying away waste and providing the body with much needed nutrients and oxygen. The heart is just as important in the spiritual sense. In scriptures, our hearts represent our inner life. We are commanded to guard our hearts because everything flows from it. Many of the issues we face physically – bad attitudes, sickness, lust, addiction, etc. – actually stem from heart issues. The Bible tells us that the heart is wicked. We are naturally hard-hearted and stubborn. Despite that, God still wants us. So how can we receive a new heart and then guard it? First, we must repent. Repentance is more than just apologizing – it is turning from our wicked behavior. Second, we must surrender to God. God is the only one who can change us. We have to surrender our hearts and let God do the work. Then we have to be careful to avoid our temptations. For example, when I was trying to be delivered from sexual sin, I had to stop listening to certain music. I had to stop watching certain movies. I had to stop hanging out with certain people. I had to be delivered from strongholds and unhealthy attachments to the people and organizations to which I had committed. In other words, I had to know my triggers and avoid them. I still have to be aware of all of these things so I can guard my heart and not fall into the same patterns. It is not easy, but God is faithful. Will you let God into your heart?

PRAYER – *Psalm 51:1-17* (NIV/ESV)

Have mercy on me, O God, according to your unfailing love; according to your great compassion blot out my transgressions. Wash away all my iniquity and cleanse me from my sin. For I know my transgressions, and my sin is always before me. Against you, you only, have I sinned and done what is evil in your sight; so you are right in your verdict and justified when you judge. Surely I was sinful at birth, sinful from the time my mother conceived me. Yet you desired faithfulness even in the womb; you taught me wisdom in that secret place. Cleanse me with hyssop, and I will be clean; wash me, and I will be whiter than snow. Let me hear joy and gladness; let the bones you have crushed rejoice. Hide your face from my sins and blot out all my iniquity. Create in me a clean heart, O God, and renew a right spirit within me. Do not cast me from your presence or take your Holy Spirit from me. Restore to me the joy of your salvation and grant me a willing spirit, to sustain me. Then I will teach transgressors your ways, so that sinners will turn back to you. Deliver me from the guilt of bloodshed, O God, you who are God my Savior, and my tongue will sing of your righteousness. Open my lips, Lord, and my mouth will declare your praise. You do not delight in sacrifice, or I would bring it; you do not take pleasure in burnt offerings. My sacrifice, O God, is a broken spirit; a broken and contrite heart you, God, will not despise. In the name of Jesus I pray. Amen.

NOTES

_____

_____

DAY 5
Find Your Identity

> *"Do not lie to each other, since you have taken off your old self with its practices and have put on the new self, which is being renewed in knowledge in the image of its Creator. Here there is no Gentile or Jew, circumcised or uncircumcised, barbarian, Scythian, slave or free, but Christ is all, and is in all." – Colossians 3:9-11 (NIV)*

> *"God created man in His own image, in the image of God He created him; male and female He created them."*
> *– Genesis 1:26-27 (NET)*

> *"But the fruit of the Spirit is love, joy, peace, forbearance, kindness, goodness, faithfulness, gentleness and self-control. Against such things there is no law." – Galatians 5:22 (NIV)*

DEVOTION

After renouncing Greek life, I had to take a period of time to figure out who I was without the letters. Greek life had been such a large part of my identity that I felt a little lost without it. Luckily, I knew that if anyone could assist me with finding my identity, it was God. After all, we are all made in God's image and God knows our innermost beings. God knows our thoughts. God knows our destiny. God knew us before we were formed in our mother's womb. God saw us and loved us!

There is an old saying that if you spend enough time with someone, you start to look, think, and act alike. That is the exact approach I had to take with God. I spent months having intentional conversations with God until God's characteristics started to rub off on me. I continued talking to God until I felt

I had clarity on who I am and what I am called to do. When you find your identity in God, you can be confident even when things don't seem to be going your way. Why? Because your identity is found in the most constant being in the universe. Most of all, finding your identity in God means you are already complete. God made you beautiful; God made you special. You don't need anyone else or anything else to complete you. Today my prayer for you is that you begin to see yourself as God sees you. I pray that you would seek God and ask for revelation about who you are and your purpose. I pray that as you seek God, you will be transformed to look more and more like the image of Christ and that you would exhibit the fruit of the Spirit. Surrender yourself so God can mold you. You are God's child. Find your identity in God alone.

PRAYER

God, today I pray that you will open my eyes so I may see myself as you see me. I am thankful that you created me in your imagine and that you believe my image is good. I pray that you would strip away all negative perceptions that I have of myself. Take away everything in me that is not like you. Help me to live in a way where people will be able to recognize me as your child, first and foremost. Help me to find my identity in you. In the name of Jesus I pray. Amen.

NOTES

_____
_____
_____
_____
_____
_____
_____

DAY 6
Why We Need A Devotional

> *"When the unclean spirit has gone out of a person, it passes through waterless places seeking rest, and finding none it says, 'I will return to my house which I came.' And when it comes, it finds the house swept and put in order. Then it goes and brings seven other spirits more evil than itself, and they enter and dwell there. And the last state of that person is worse than the first."*
> *– Matthew 12:43-45 (ESV)*

DEVOTION

Once we have been delivered from something, whatever that something may be, there will be a part of us missing. When I left Greek life, it seemed like I had so much time on my hands, and surely that was to be expected. After all, being Greek consumed me – I had pledged and taken an oath to give the organization my everything. When I renounced, I left behind some of my "friends." I wasn't getting invited to as many parties; I didn't have to plan as many events. I felt a little empty. And my emptiness could have become open ground for the enemy.

Once we have been delivered, it is possible for the evil spirit to come back seven times stronger. We can take time to clean our houses so that they look clean on the outside; but the reality is if we are empty spiritually there is room for the enemy to come back, leaving us worse than we were before. So how do we ensure that we are being filled with good things? With what do we fill ourselves? The word of God is the answer. Spend time reading God's word; Spend time praying to God. Surround yourself with people who will lift you and expose you to more positive parts of life. Ask the Lord to fill you with the Holy Spirit.

PRAYER

Dear Lord, thank you for removing everything from me that is contrary to your will. I pray now that you would fill me with your Holy Spirit. I pray that I would be so filled by you that there is no room for any evil spirits to take residence in me. I declare that I am your child. I declare that you are the ruler and the Lord of my life. I ask that you would send positive people into my life who will pour into me spiritually. Let my life not just appear to be clean and in order on the outside, but allow me to be changed, purified, and filled with the Holy Spirit from the inside out. In the name of Jesus I pray. Amen.

NOTES

DAY 7
Rest In The Presence Of God

"He says, 'Be still, and know that I am God; I will be exalted among the nations, I will be exalted in the earth.'"
– Psalm 46:10 (NIV)

DEVOTION

At times you have to be by yourself and spend time with the Lord. Today I encourage you to spend at least five minutes alone with God. You won't find a prompted prayer, but I have included the name of a song that you can listen to while you meditate. Talk to God about whatever you like. There are lines on the next page if you like to journal. I hope you find rest for your soul.

SONG

Away From the Noise – Israel Houghton and New Breed

JOURNAL ENTRY:

Dear God,

DAY 8
A Good Thing, Or A God Thing?

> *"'I have the right to do anything,' you say – but not everything is beneficial. 'I have the right to do anything' – but not everything is constructive." – 1 Corinthians 10:23 (NIV)*

> *"For you are free, yet you are God's slaves, so don't use your freedom as an excuse to do evil." – 1 Peter 2:16 (NLT)*

> *"This false teaching is like a little yeast that spreads through the whole batch of dough!" – Galatians 5:9 (NLT)*

DEVOTION

Just because something is good does not necessarily mean it's ordained by God. There were many times in the Bible where people were saying or doing "good" things – performing miracles, winning battles, etc. However, they were steadily leading people astray. Even if something is good, it doesn't mean we have to do it or that we should do it, especially if the good masks bad things. Community service is good; fellowship is good; desiring to make good grades is good; and all of those things being good were the main reasons people encouraged me to remain in Greek life. However, I came to the realization that all of the "good" things that were offered could be offered or done without the negative parts that came along with Greek life. No, not all of my experiences were bad: however, turning a blind eye to the seemingly small bad things is what gets us caught up in things contrary to God's will. It's almost like a bad relationship. We continue with the relationship, thinking things will get better, saying things like "it's not all bad." Meanwhile, we are becoming more and more attached and intertwined, making it more difficult to move on even after we finally come to our senses. When it comes to something being a God thing, we have to be discerning. We have to ask if God is getting the glory out of what we are doing or is the glory going to something or someone else. We have to ask if what we are doing contradicts Godly principles and standards. We have to ask if we are putting so much of our time and energy into these "good" things that we no longer have time to give ourselves to God's agenda. If we seek God first, we will be granted wisdom for whether or not we should spend our time with what "seems" good.

PRAYER
Dear Lord, help me to be able to distinguish the good things from the God things. Open my eyes to be able to tell the difference between tests and trials that I must work through and things that are contrary to your word — those things I should run from. Help me to know my gifts so that I can know what I am called to do in this world. Let my actions bring YOU glory! In the name of Jesus I pray. Amen.

NOTES

DAY 9
Putting God First

> *"You shall have no other gods before me." – Exodus 20:3 (NIV)*

> *"Do not worship any other God, for the Lord, whose name is Jealous, is a jealous God." – Exodus 34:14 (NIV)*

> *"Jesus replied: "Love the Lord your God with all your heart and with all your soul and with all your mind."*
> *– Matthew 22:37 (NIV)*

> *"Anyone who loves their father or mother more than me is not worthy of me; anyone who loves their son or daughter more than me is not worthy of me. Whoever does not take up their cross and follow me is not worthy of me." – Matthew 10:37-38 (NIV)*

DEVOTION

Growing up in the church, I often heard "put God first." Jesus says that the greatest commandment is to love God with all of our heart. I knew I was not supposed to put anything before God. Yet, for some reason when I pledged, I saw nothing wrong with channeling a Greek god during certain ceremonies. I saw nothing wrong with giving the sorority all of my time, all of my love, and all of my money. I very quickly put the sorority before the God who had been so faithful to me. The sorority consumed me; and while I continued being active in my home church, it was very clear that my heart was not seeking God. How could I find time to put God first when I was "always wearing my letters"? It was the sorority first and everything else came after it. Greek organizations are constantly getting the glory. They have special songs at weddings; they have special ceremonies at funerals. People allegedly go to another chapter after they die. "Did you pledge?" was often the first question people asked me at most events. When good things happen in our lives, instead of giving God glory, we throw up Greek signs or symbols that really have nothing to do with our accomplishments. Matthew 6:24 says "No one can serve two masters. Either you will hate the one and love the other, or you will be devoted to the one and despise the other. You cannot serve both God and money." Although this scripture pertains to money, the principle can apply to other areas of our lives. As we juggle all of life's responsibilities, we have to ask ourselves "what do we serve more?" Have you put God on the back burner?

CHALLENGE
We must train ourselves to honor God in everything we do. Colossians 3:23 tells us that no matter what we are doing, we should work at it with all our heart as though working for the Lord. Throughout the day, take note of who you are honoring through your actions, through your words, and through your thoughts. Is God getting the glory? Are you listening for God throughout the day? Are you submitting to God's will on your job? While at school? While at home? Do you only think about God while in the physical building of your church? Reflect on what you notice and make an action plan for how you can put God first in every situation.

PRAYER
Dear Lord, I repent for every time I have placed something, or someone else, before you. I am thankful that even when I go astray, you wait patiently for me to return. Today, I put you back in your rightful place as number one in my life. I desire to be totally committed to you. Allow me to show you that you are first as I devote the majority of my time to you as I communicate with you; as I obey your will; and as I serve your people. My soul longs for you and you alone Lord. In the name of Jesus I pray. Amen.

DAY 10
Love Your Neighbor

"By this everyone will know that you are my disciples, if you love one another." – John 13:35 (NIV)

"And the second [greatest commandment] is like it: 'Love your neighbor as yourself.'" – Matthew 22:39 (NIV)

"And now these three remain faith hope and love. But the greatest of these is love." – 1 Corinthians 13:13 (NIV)

"Do not lie to each other, since you have taken off your old self with its practices and have put on the new self, which is being renewed in knowledge in the image of its Creator. Here there is no Gentile or Jew, circumcised or uncircumcised, barbarian, Scythian, slave or free, but Christ is all, and is in all" – Colossians 3:9-11 (NIV)

"Treat everyone with high regard: love the brotherhood of believers, fear God, honor the king." – 1 Peter 2:17 (BSB)

DEVOTION

The second greatest commandment is to love our neighbor as ourselves. I had a hard time figuring out how I showed love to my neighbor while I was in a Greek letter organization. While I certainly had sisters and brothers whom I loved, there was also an entire population of people who had to be excluded because they were not "Greek material." There were people who weren't college educated; people who didn't meet the GPA requirement; people who the current chapter members just didn't like (let's be real about it), etc. The love experienced by those in the sorority was not extended to those who didn't make it in – and my God is a God of inclusivity. Anyone can participate in God's Kingdom if they so choose. In addition, my journey to and through Greek life did not always exude love – hazing rituals, constant pressure to prove myself worthy of the letters I wore, and the stress of not being shown love if others thought my process wasn't hard enough. I think about the things I went through in order to be shown "love" and I've decided that it really wasn't love at all. Love does not end because I no longer wear certain letters. Love is not proud. Love is not belittling people who are likely more qualified than I am. I appreciate having a God who loves me unconditionally; a God who loves me and desires to be with me despite my imperfections. All activities in which I choose to participate need to allow me the opportunity to share the love of God with everyone I encounter, not just a select few.

PRAYER

Dear Lord, I thank you for showing me your love, a real love. I thank you for loving me enough to send your only Son to die for my sins and the sins of all mankind. Thank you for offering an opportunity for all of us to be covered under the blood of Jesus, an equal opportunity. I pray that you would give me a compassionate heart, that I would be able to share your love with others. I pray that I would make people feel included, and that I would be comfortable with interacting with all types of people. Help me to not exclude those who don't look or act like me, but help me to be able to love others unconditionally. Help me to see others as you see them. In the name of Jesus I pray. Amen.

NOTES

_____

_____

_____

_____

DAY 11
Don't Deceive Your Brother

"If your very own brother, or your son or daughter, or the wife you love, or your closest friend secretly enticed you, saying "Let us go and worship other gods" (gods that neither you nor your ancestors have known, gods of the peoples around you, whether near or far, from one end of the land to the other), do not yield to them or listen to them. Show them no pity. Do not spare them or shield them."
– Deuteronomy 13:6-9 (NIV)

"Therefore let us not pass judgment on one another any longer, but rather decide never to put a stumbling block or hindrance in the way of a brother." – Romans 14:13 (NIV)

"You are the light of the world. A town built on a hill cannot be hidden. Neither do people light a lamp and put it under a bowl. Instead they put it on its stand, and it gives light to everyone in the house. In the same way, let your light shine before others, that they may see your good deeds and glorify your Father in heaven."
– Matthew 5:14-16 (NIV)

DEVOTION

Whether we know it or not, our actions have influence on others. You may have younger siblings or family members who look up to you; mentees who look to you as a role model; or friends who come to you for advice. Since so many people are watching, we must consider how our actions impact others. Our actions might bring someone closer to Christ or in the alternative cause them to stumble. Did you know that in the Old Testament the penalty for enticing your brothers and sisters to serve other gods was death? Most people don't intentionally lead people astray; but, as leaders, we can make people believe that certain behaviors are okay. This is especially true for people who are weaker in their faith. I am thankful that God delivered me from certain behaviors before my younger sisters or my future children were able to replicate them. However, I still feel saddened by the number of people I was able to influence before God opened my eyes. Those behaviors are not specific to secret societies but anything that is contrary to God – drunkenness, sexual immorality, etc. I know you might be thinking, "this is my life, I'm going to do what I want." But our lives are not our own! We cannot be selfish! We were created to bring God glory and we were commanded to love one another. Part of loving one another is looking out for one another's best interests. When thinking about whether you should be doing something, ask yourself if you would want your children, your younger siblings, younger family members, doing the same thing. Ask yourself if there is any way that your actions could take you or others from God. We are supposed to be the light of the world; the light that others may see God through us and glorify Him. We must care about our brothers and sisters more than we care about our own freedoms. If there's a chance your actions might give the wrong impression to your brother or sister, save them some confusion and just don't do it.

PRAYER
Dear Lord, I repent for being selfish and not considering others with some of the decisions I have made. I repent for some of my actions which may have led people away from you instead of drawing them to you. I am so happy that you did not repay me for my actions with the death that I deserved. Today, I commit to being all in for you. Today, I commit to consider how my actions impact your children. I hope that my change in behavior will cause someone to want to know you more. In the name of Jesus I pray. Amen.

DAY 12
Be Gentle With Your Neighbor

> *"And the Lord's servant must not be quarrelsome but must be kind to everyone, able to teach, not resentful. Opponents must be gently instructed, in the hope that God will grant them repentance leading them to a knowledge of the truth, and that they will come to their senses and escape from the trap of the devil, who has taken them captive to do his will." – 2 Timothy 2:24-26 (NIV)*

> *"Who are you to judge someone else's servant? To their own master, servants stand or fall. And they will stand, for the Lord is able to make them stand. One person considers one day more sacred than another; another considers every day alike. Each of them should be fully convinced in their own mind." – Romans 14: 4-5 (NIV)*

DEVOTION

When I was first called out of Greek life, I tried to share what had been revealed to me hoping it would cause others to flee from Greek life as well. Looking back, I really tried too hard and turned a lot of people off from listening to me altogether. Since then, I have realized that it's not my job to turn people around. Instead, I can start by being transparent about my experience and ask God to do the rest. There was a time when people tried to talk to me about how Christian life didn't line up with Greek life; and I was so wrapped up in it that I would become angry because I couldn't see what they saw. Furthermore, if I did see what they saw, I wasn't ready to accept it. It took God fully opening my eyes in a way that I could no longer ignore the truth. Even though my eyes were opened and my convictions could not be ignored, I had to learn that my convictions are not everyone else's convictions.

Only God can change people's hearts. I can't change people and neither can you. We can, however, speak the truth in love, provide advice when asked, and pray that others will be led to repentance. My advice to you is that you be patient with your friends or family who may not be living the way you think they should. This is general advice for any situation. Seek God and be an example of what you think God wants in a follower. Pray that they will come into the knowledge of God for themselves before it is too late.

PRAYER

Lord, help me to stay in my place, knowing that I am not God and that I do not have to try to play God. That job is taken. Teach me how to be gentle and patient with everyone, just as patient as you are with me. Allow me to be a walking example of your grace and mercy. Send more of your disciples into the world to reach the people I can't. I take a step back and allow you to take full control. I trust you to soften hearts and bring others into the knowledge of your truth. And Lord, if I have things wrong in my own mind, teach me the right way. Soften my heart. Make me more like you. In the name of Jesus I pray. Amen.

NOTES

DAY 13
Love Yourself

> *"And the second [greatest commandment] is like it: 'Love your neighbor as yourself.'"* – Matthew 22:39 (NIV)

> *"For you created my inmost being; you knit me together in my mother's womb. I praise you because I am fearfully and wonderfully made; your works are wonderful, I know that full well. My frame was not hidden from you when I was made in the secret place, when I was woven together in the depths of the earth. Your eyes saw my unformed body; all the days ordained for me were written in your book before one of them came to be. How precious to me are your thoughts, O God. They cannot be numbered!"*
> – Psalm 139:13-17 (NIV/NLT)

> *"For we are God's handiwork, created in Christ Jesus to do good works, which God prepared in advance for us to do."*
> – Ephesians 2:10 (NIV)

DEVOTION

Living in a world of social media, one can easily fall into a state of feeling inadequate. It is easy to feel like you are not pretty enough, smart enough, or rich enough – sometimes people will tell you as much. Today, I want to remind you that you are fearfully and wonderfully made. You were created to do good works. You are not your mistakes. You are beautiful. You are intelligent. You are gifted. You are forgiven. You are chosen. You are loved. You are enough, even without man-made labels. Now please understand, these affirmations are not to make you arrogant! Please do not walk around with your nose in the air. I just think it's so important to learn to love ourselves.

We are often much harder on ourselves than anyone else. We won't forgive ourselves for mistakes we have made. Often, we think we should have more, or do more, or know more. Loving ourselves is what grants us the capability to love others. When we love ourselves, we do not have to be jealous of other people; we can rejoice in the successes of others because we don't have to envy their accomplishments. When we love ourselves, we are happier; we are more confident. Then we can encourage others to love themselves as well. Start loving yourself today!

CHALLENGE
Today, I encourage you to write down five positive affirmations about yourself. Write down scriptures that confirm those affirmations! Speak them over yourself daily.

PRAYER
Dear Lord, thank you for showing me that I am worthy of love. Teach me, Lord, how to love myself, to accept myself, and to forgive myself, so that I may know how to truly love others. Help me to see myself as you see me. Cleanse my heart from all bitterness and jealousy. In the name of Jesus I pray. Amen.

NOTES
_____
_____
_____
_____
_____
_____
_____

DAY 14
Rest In The Presence Of God

He says, "Be still, and know that I am God; I will be exalted among the nations, I will be exalted in the earth.
– Psalm 46:10 (NIV)

"You will keep in perfect peace those whose minds are steadfast, because they trust in you." – Isaiah 26:3 (NIV)

DEVOTION

At times you have to be by yourself and spend time with the Lord. Today I encourage you to spend at least ten minutes alone with God. You won't find a prompted prayer, but I have included the name of a song that you can listen to while you meditate. Talk to God about whatever you like. There are lines on the next page if you like to journal. I hope you find rest for your soul.

SONG
The Call – Isabel Davis

JOURNAL ENTRY:

Dear God,

DAY 15
Comfortable Christianity

"But the king said to Araunah, 'No, but I will certainly buy it from you for a price. I will not offer burnt offerings to the Lord my God that which cost me nothing.' So David purchased the threshing floor and the oxen for fifty shekels of silver."
– *2 Samuel 24:24 (AMP)*

"Jesus answered, 'If you want to be perfect, go, sell your possessions and give to the poor, and you will have treasure in heaven. Then come, follow me.' When the young man heard this, he went away sad, because he had great wealth." – Matthew 19:21-22 (NIV)

"As they were walking along the road, a man said to him, 'I will follow you wherever you go.' Jesus replies, 'Foxes have dens and birds have nests, but the Son of Man has no place to lay his head.' He said to another man, 'Follow me.' But he replied, 'Lord, first let me go and bury my father.' Jesus said to him, 'Let the dead bury their own dead, but you go and proclaim the kingdom of God.' Still another said, 'I will follow you, Lord; but first let me go back and say goodbye to my family.' Jesus replied, 'No one who puts a hand to the plow and looks back is fit for service in the kingdom of God.'" – Luke 9:57-62 (NIV)

"Then Jesus told his disciples, 'If anyone would come after me, let him deny himself and take up his cross and follow me. For whoever would save his life will lose it, but whoever loses his life for my sake will find it. For what will it profit a man if he gains the whole

world and forfeits his soul? Or what shall a man give in return for his soul?'" – Matthew 16:24-26 (ESV)

DEVOTION

In 2015, Caleb Seifu released an awesome book called COMFORTABLE CHRISTIANITY. The book made me realize how good we have it in America. Although theologies and interpretations may differ, we worship with the majority of those in America. We can be bold about our belief in Jesus Christ without suffering much persecution. How would we act if the tables were turned? Would we still follow Jesus if it was not the popular thing to do? Are there ways we have compromised our faith in order to fit in with the world? Are there things, or even people, in your life who you put before God? If God said to you, "leave that or them, and follow me," would you do it? Or would you walk away sad like the man in Matthew 19:21-22? Sometimes we must analyze our priorities and see where God really lines up. Today I encourage you to think about the foundation of your faith. Are you really rooted in Jesus? How do you show it? Let's stop being comfortable Christians and become true followers of Jesus Christ. Following Jesus will require us to get out of our comfort zones. It will cost us something. What would you give up to follow God?

PRAYER

Lord, I repent for not being willing to give up my all to follow you. I thank you for the pleasures you have given me in this life; but even if I didn't have them, I would still be happy to serve you. You thought enough of me to leave the comforts of heaven, come to this sinful world, to die on a cross just to save me from my sins. The least I can do is serve you wholeheartedly. Today, I commit to serving you through the good and the bad. I will not give you what costs me nothing. I choose you over everything I have gained in this world. I choose you over my own comforts. You are my reward. In the name of Jesus I pray. Amen.

DAY 16
Pleasing God vs. Pleasing Man

"Am I now trying to win the approval of human beings, or of God? Or am I trying to please people? If I were still trying to please people, I would not be a servant of Christ."
– Galatians 1:10 (NIV)

"Enter through the narrow gate. For wide is the gate and broad is the road that leads to destruction, and many enter through it. But small is the gate and narrow the road that leads to life, and only a few find it." – Matthew 7:13-14 (NIV)

DEVOTION

I used to find myself in arguments with people who didn't understand some of the spiritual decisions I have made. I would go back and forth with them, but I eventually realized that my decisions are not about them. Now my hope is that my decisions, as with any deliverance story, may bring others to repentance or maybe deter others from making the same mistakes I did. However, at the end of the day, my decisions are just that – mine. These decisions are between me and my God. These are the steps I made to show that I was obedient to what God called me to do. If God commands you to do something, you cannot be sidetracked or swayed by the opinions of others. You also can't be afraid to tell people how God is directing you. We are servants of Christ, and it is God's command that we are taught to follow. This is not always going to be doing what is popular in the eyesight of man. On the contrary, following God will probably cause us to go against the grain. It is not always easy; but we can't let anyone, not even our own biological family, dissuade us from being obedient to God. God's opinion is the only one that matters and obedience to God leads to eternal life.

PRAYER

God, please deliver me from the fear of man's judgment. My desire is to please you and you alone. Help me to know and follow your voice. I realize that if I am to follow you, I may have to leave some people behind. I might have to make the unpopular decision. Help me to be satisfied with you. Lord, if you are pleased with what I do, nothing else matters. In the name of Jesus I pray. Amen.

NOTES

DAY 17
Am I Still A Christian If...?

"I know your deeds, that you are neither cold nor hot. I wish you were either one or the other! So, because you are lukewarm – neither hot nor cold – I am about to spit you out of my mouth."
– Revelation 3:15-16 (NIV)

"The Lord says: 'These people come near to me with their mouth and honor me with their lips, but their hearts are far from me. Their worship of me is based on merely human rules they have been taught.'" – Isaiah 29:13 (NIV)

DEVOTION

I've been asked many times if someone can still be a Christian if they are in a Greek organization. Some ask if they are still going to heaven if they are in a Greek organization. I don't have a heaven or a hell to put people in, but I think a better question is "what is God saying to me?" As believers, we should not be skirting around trying to figure out how close we can get to the sin line before we get into trouble. The Israelites, the Pharisees, and the Sadducees all thought they were doing wonderfully because they were doing their best to follow the laws, but none of that mattered because their hearts were hard and God knew it. Following God is not about following rules so that we can self-righteously say we are pleasing God. Following God is about surrendering our hearts. It's about trusting God to know what's best for us rather than following our flesh. It's about being patient with ourselves. It's about listening to what God is saying, living according to God's word, and expecting a reward for our obedience. Don't ask "can I still be a Christian if I do this?" Instead ask "is this going to glorify God?" If the answer is "no", maybe you shouldn't do it.

PRAYER

God, please change my heart so that I won't be like the Pharisees who were more concerned with following rules than surrendering their hearts to you. Transform me so that I won't seek to do the bare minimum as a Christian. I want to be all in. I don't want to obey you because I am afraid of the consequences. I want to obey you because I love you. I want to obey you to show that I appreciate the sacrifices you have made for me. I obey you because you saved me. I surrender to you. In the name of Jesus I pray. Amen.

NOTES

DAY 18
The Devil Made Me Do It

"No temptation has overtaken you except what is common to mankind. And God is faithful; he will not let you be tempted beyond what you can bear. But when you are tempted, he will also provide a way out so that you can endure it."
– 1 Corinthians 10:13 (NIV)

Submit yourselves therefore to God. Resist the devil, and he will flee from you. – James 4: 7 (ESV)

DEVOTION

I never quite understood the phrase "the devil made me do it." Sure the devil tempts us; but as I reflect on every poor decision I have made, there was no demon putting a gun to my head, forcing me to give in. No, there was just me – me choosing to party; me choosing to engage in sexual sin; and me choosing to lie to cover up the things I was doing. Each one of the poor decisions I made was rooted in my own insecurity or some door that I had opened and failed to close. Each poor decision I made came from my failure to be completely surrendered to God. Each poor decision I made came from me choosing myself, and what my flesh wanted, over God's plan. The devil may have exploited my insecurities, but I have no one to blame for my mistakes but me – me and my sinful nature. I can't give the devil that much control, that much credit. It's time for all of us take responsibility for our actions. We can't blame anyone but ourselves. Accepting responsibility is one of the first steps to becoming whole. Admit your mistakes and take them to the one who knows how to handle our sinful nature – Jesus Christ.

PRAYER

Lord, help me to take responsibility for the things I have done. I understand that admitting my own wrongs may be the first step to being made whole. Reveal my insecurities to me so that I won't be naïve to where I may be weakest. Strengthen me so that I might take the escape route when temptation comes my way. Teach me how to resist the devil so that he will flee. In the name of Jesus I pray. Amen.

NOTES

DAY 19
Dust Yourself Off And Try Again

"Therefore there is now no condemnation for those who are in Christ Jesus, because through Christ Jesus the law of the Spirit who gives life has set you free from the law of sin and death."
– *Romans 8:1 (NIV)*

"But he said to me, 'My grace is sufficient for you, for my power is made perfect in weakness.' Therefore I will boast all the more gladly about my weaknesses, so that Christ's power may rest on me."
– *2 Corinthians 12:9 (NIV)*

". . . for though the righteous man may fall seven times, they rise again, but the wicked stumble when calamity strikes."
– *Proverbs 24:16 (NIV)*

DEVOTION

"If at first you don't succeed, try, try again." This is a lesson we learn as children. A lesson we can utilize in adulthood as well. Leaving certain things behind isn't easy. Sometimes you will miss what you used to do. You might even revert to some of your old ways. It might be hard but don't give up! God's grace covers you. The Holy Spirit can strengthen you in your time of weakness. We just have to realize that we can't do it by ourselves. It is okay for us to fail. If we never failed, we wouldn't need Jesus. It is not, however, okay for us to just remain in our failures and unfaithfulness. We can't give up. We can't decide to be taken over by our sinful nature. If you fall, get back up! Try again. Repent and forgive yourself. Allow grace to abound in your life.

PRAYER

Dear Lord, thank you for being an all-powerful God who has enough grace to cover my sins. Lord, thank you for sending your son to cover the sins I have committed and the ones I have yet to commit. Lord, when I fall, help me to have the strength to start again. Do not let me become paralyzed by disappointment but send me reminders that your grace is sufficient for even a person like me. In the name of Jesus I pray. Amen.

NOTES

_____
_____
_____
_____
_____
_____
_____
_____
_____
_____
_____
_____
_____
_____
_____
_____
_____
_____
_____
_____

DAY 20
Dealing With Consequences

Then David said to Nathan, "I have sinned against the LORD." Nathan answered, "The LORD has taken away your sin. You will not die. But what you did caused the LORD's enemies to lose all respect for him. For this reason the son who was born to you will die." Then Nathan went home. And the LORD caused the son of David and Bathsheba, Uriah's widow, to be very sick. David prayed to God for the baby. David fasted and went into his house and stayed there, lying on the ground all night. The elders of David's family came to him and tried to pull him up from the ground, but he refused to get up or to eat food with them. On the seventh day the baby died. David's servants were afraid to tell him that the baby was dead. They said, "Look, we tried to talk to David while the baby was alive, but he refused to listen to us. If we tell him the baby is dead, he may do something awful." When David saw his servants whispering, he knew that the baby was dead. So he asked them, "Is the baby dead?" They answered, "Yes, he is dead." Then David got up from the floor, washed himself, put lotions on, and changed his clothes. Then he went into the LORD's house to worship. After that, he went home and asked for something to eat. His servants gave him some food, and he ate. David's servants said to him, "Why are you doing this? When the baby was still alive, you fasted and you cried. Now that the baby is dead, you get up and eat food." David said, "While the baby was still alive, I fasted, and I cried. I thought, 'Who knows? Maybe the LORD will feel sorry for me and let the baby live.' But now that

the baby is dead, why should I fast? I can't bring him back to life. Someday I will go to him, but he cannot come back to me."
– 2 Samuel 12:13-23 (NCV)

DEVOTION

We can't talk about God's grace without talking about consequences. You may repent. You may be delivered. And that's great! However, you may still have to deal with the consequences of your actions. In the text for today, David committed a sin and the consequence of that sin was the death of his son. David fasted in an attempt to pray away the consequence, but the damage had already been done. David's sin had already caused God's reputation to be ruined. When David learned that his son died, he got up determined to live in a way that would allow him to see his son again in heaven. Often times, we sin but we don't want to deal with the effects of sin. Some of us even sin, fully expecting for God to forgive us. We take grace for granted and then think we have been wronged when faced with the consequences of what we did. When we make our beds, we have to lie in them. Dealing with our consequences may require us to experience shame, mental or physical troubles, or hurt of those closest to us. The list could go on and on. I don't say this to scare you (that much) but I don't want you to be naïve. God is definitely faithful to forgive us of our sins. God may throw our sins into the sea of forgetfulness, but the world does not. When we fall, let's handle the consequences with humility and commit to doing better the next time.

PRAYER

Lord, I thank you for being a God who will discipline me, but not condemn me. I know that we all have sinned and fallen short of the glory. When I fall short, I pray that I would handle the consequences with humility. I don't want to take grace for granted. I appreciate the grace you have extended to me. When I must suffer a consequence, let me learn a lesson so that I will not have to suffer again or deal with something worse. In the name of Jesus I pray. Amen.

NOTES

DAY 21
Rest In The Presence Of God

"He says, 'Be still, and know that I am God; I will be exalted among the nations, I will be exalted in the earth.'"
– *Psalm 46:10 (NIV)*

"You will keep in perfect peace those whose minds are steadfast, because they trust in you." – Isaiah 26:3 (NIV)

"Come to me, all you who are weary and burdened, and I will give you rest. Take my yoke upon you and learn from me, for I am gentle and humble in heart, and you will find rest for your souls. For my yoke is easy and my burden is light."
– *Matthew 11:28-30 (NIV)*

DEVOTION

At times you have to be by yourself and spend time with the Lord. Today I encourage you to spend at least fifteen minutes alone with God. You won't find a prompted prayer, but I have included a list of songs that you can listen to while you meditate. Talk to God about whatever you like. There are lines on the next page if you like to journal. I hope you find rest for your soul.

SONGS
Before the Throne – Shekinah Glory
Forever at Your Feet – Tasha Cobbs

JOURNAL ENTRY:

Dear God,

DAY 22
Fruit of the Spirit vs. Fruit of the Flesh

"The acts of the flesh are obvious: sexual immortality, impurity and debauchery; idolatry and witchcraft; hatred, discord, and jealousy, fits of rage, selfish ambition, dissensions, factions and envy; drunkenness, orgies, and the like. I warn you, as I did before, that those who live like this will not inherit the kingdom of God. But the fruit of the Spirit is love, joy, peace, forbearance, kindness, goodness, faithfulness, gentleness and self-control. Against such things there is no law." – Galatians 5:19-22 (NIV)

DEVOTION

Sometimes we make it so difficult to determine what is good and what is not. This scripture, very plainly, outlines the fruit of the Spirit; it also outlines the fruit of the flesh. What fruit is growing in your life?

PRAYER

Dear Lord, help me to be full of your Spirit. I desire to have more love, more joy, more peace, more patience, more kindness, more goodness, more faithfulness, more gentleness, and more self-control in all areas of my life. Take everything out of me that is not like you. In the name of Jesus I pray. Amen.

NOTES

_____
_____
_____
_____
_____

DAY 23
Why Me?

> *"And we know that God causes all things to work together for good for those who love God, to those who are called according to His purpose." – Romans 8:28 (NASB)*

DEVOTION

At times I've wondered why God allowed me to go through the things that I have. Why didn't God just stop me from messing up? Why me? But I heard a song by Fantasia and Dennis Reed that says, "I am who I am today because God used my mistakes. He worked it for my good like no one else ever could. It was necessary." As I meditated on the words of that song, I begin to wonder, why not me? Why can't I be used to bring God glory? Why can't I be a testimony of God's redemptive power? I have made mistakes – many of them. I have passed some tests and I have failed others. Instead of hiding behind my mistakes, I am choosing to use them to bring God glory and, hopefully, keep others from making the same mistakes I did. I am happy to serve a God who allows me to make my own decisions. When I don't make the right choice, I am happy that God can still use my mistakes for the good of The Kingdom. If God can use me, I'm sure God can use you, if you'll allow it. Don't ask "why me?" You should ask, "why not me?"

PRAYER

Lord, I thank you for being a God who can use my mistakes. I thank you for being a God who is able to work all things together for my good. Show me how I can use the tests I have been through as a testimony to bring you all glory, honor, and praise. In the name of Jesus I pray. Amen.

DAY 24
Confidently Christian

"For I am confident of this very thing, that He who began a good work in you will perfect it until the day of Christ Jesus."
– Philippians 1:6 (NASB)

"Be strong and courageous, do not be afraid or tremble at them, for the Lord your God is the one who goes with you He will not fail you or forsake you." – Deuteronomy 31:6 (NASB)

"SO commit yourself to God completely. Reach out your hands to Him for help. Get rid of all of the sin you have. Don't let anything that is evil stay in your tent. Then you can face others without feeling any shame. You can stand firm without being afraid. You can be sure you will forget your troubles. They will be like water that has flowed on by. Life will be brighter than the sun at noon. And darkness will become like morning. You will be secure because there is hope. You will look around you and find a safe place to rest. You will lie down, and no one will make you afraid. Many people will want you to show them your favor. But sinful people won't find what they are looking for. They won't be able to escape. All they can hope for is to die." – Job 11:13-20 (NIrV)

"Therefore, my beloved brethren, be steadfast, immovable, always abounding in the work of the Lord, knowing that your toil is not in vain in the Lord." – 1 Corinthians 15:58 (NIV)

DEVOTION

I remember being afraid to tell certain people that I had renounced my membership from the sorority. I removed my photos off social media quietly – only because I didn't want that to be the first thing people saw about me. I grew tired of having to have a back and forth conversation when people realized I had renounced. Why couldn't I just be me? It probably took two years before I became completely comfortable with having the conversation about my decision with others – a decision that I could finally explain biblically and spiritually. When I was Greek, I told the world. My lifestyle, well, the more glamourous parts, was everywhere for the world to see. I was so bold with telling people I was Greek; yet, I would sometimes get nervous when I had to witness to someone about Jesus. I'd struggle with sharing scriptures on social media. What would people think? Well, it should never be this way. We should be confident in our choice to follow God. We should be bold and excited when it comes to spreading the gospel. Today I encourage you to be a confident Christian. Be secure in your faith. Don't be ashamed of your testimony. The world desperately needs transparency.

PRAYER

Lord, teach me how to be confident in my decision to follow you. Teach me how to spread your gospel; to live as your disciple; and to expect that you will complete me. I know that because of your love, I can be secure. I don't have to fear. I don't have to be ashamed. I know that my work is not in vain. I trust you and the plan that you have for my life. In the name of Jesus I pray. Amen.

NOTES

_____

_____

_____

DAY 25
Close The Door

"But each person is tempted when he is lured and enticed by his own desire." – James 1:14 (ESV)

"Submit yourselves therefore to God. Resist the devil, and he will flee from you." – James 4:7 (ESV)

"When an impure spirit comes out of a person, it goes into the desert seeking rest and does not find it. Then it says, 'I will return to the house I left.' When it arrives, it finds the house unoccupied, swept clean and put in order. Then it goes and takes with it seven other spirits more wicked than itself, and they go in and live there. And the final condition of that person is worse than the first. That is how it will be with this wicked generation."
– Matthew 12:43-45 (NLT)

"No temptation has overtaken you that is not common to man. God is faithful, and he will not let you be tempted beyond your ability, but with the temptation He will also provide the way of escape, that you may be able to endure it."
– 1 Corinthians 10:13 (ESV)

DEVOTION
Often, we fall back into the same cycle because we don't change our surroundings after we have been delivered. We ask the Lord to deliver us from drugs or alcohol, but we remain in places where those things are kept or offered. We want to be delivered from pornography and masturbation, but we continue to keep our phones and laptops close by at night or otherwise when

we are alone. We ask the Lord to break us from an unhealthy relationship, but we don't want to block the person. We continue to entertain their conversations; in fact, we pray that they'll contact us just to see if they still care. We want to be delivered from food but won't push back the plate. If these are not your personal struggle, just insert your own personal sins or weaknesses – we all have or have had something. After God has delivered you, it is your job to make sure you don't fall into the same trap again. In fact after we have been delivered, we have to be extra careful to fill ourselves with the Word of God because the devil will come back even stronger than before. Take proactive steps to close the door to your past life. Say no to certain parties; hit the block button on your devices; throw away things that remind you of your sin. Find an accountability partner; push back the plate; pray when you get weak. Now there may come a time when you are strong enough to be around your former temptation but don't be too proud to admit when you are weak. Close the door. Refuse to go back to the way you once were. And if closing the door is too abstract, I have another word for you…RUN. RUN FOR YOUR LIFE.

PRAYER

Dear Lord, today I pray for strength to close the door to my past sins. I do not want to go back to the way I was. I pray that I will be strong enough to flee from sin rather than give in to it. I pray that I will be more concerned about living a life for you, instead of wondering what people will say about me when I don't do the things I once did. I pray that you would fill me up so that there will be no room for the enemy to operate in my life. In the precious name of Jesus I pray. Amen.

NOTES

_____

_____

DAY 26
Do Your Research

"Be diligent to present yourself approved to God as a worker who does not need to be ashamed, rightly dividing the word of truth."
– 2 Timothy 2:15 (NKJV)

"Beloved, do not believe every spirit, but test the spirits to see whether they are from God, for many false prophets have gone out into the world." – 1 John 4:1 (ESV)

"Do not conform to the pattern of this world, but be transformed by the renewing of your mind. Then you will be able to test and approve what God's will is – his good, pleasing, and perfect will."
– Romans 12:2 (NIV)

"If any of you lacks wisdom, let him ask God, who gives generously to all without finding fault, and it will be given to you."
– James 1:5 (NIV)

DEVOTION

It is so important for us to do unbiased research before we commit ourselves to anything. I can't count the number of times I have rushed into something without asking questions only to end up in a mess. When I wanted to be Greek, I looked at information that told me it was okay to be in a Greek organization. When I wanted to stay Greek I looked at more information that told me it was okay to remain. It wasn't until God opened my eyes and heart that I begin to unbiasedly compare what I was doing to what God commands. I encourage you to do your research first, not after things start to seem weird or go astray. In doing so, you may prevent a lot of unnecessary heartache, break ups, setbacks, etc. Of course, see what the Bible says but also look to other historical and other reliable resources. I recommend doing more than just talking to other people about your thoughts (although it's good to get other opinions) but to study for yourself. Still, there is some wisdom and discernment that will come only by getting closer to God. So while I encourage you to research, I most of all encourage you to nurture your relationship with the Lord so that the Holy Spirit will convict you and grant you with discernment when determining whether or not something is of God.

PRAYER

Dear God, please soften my heart so that I will receive whatever wisdom you want to give me. Your word says your people perish due to lack of knowledge. I do not want to be one of those people. Instead, I want to test something before I rush into it. Give me a spirit of discernment so that I can flee from those things that don't line up with your will. Most of all Lord, I want to know you. I know that when I seek you, everything else will be added to me. In the name of Jesus I pray, Amen.

NOTES

DAY 27
Join The Team

". . . that if you confess with your mouth the Lord Jesus and believe in your heart that God has raised Him from the dead, you will be saved. For with the heart one believes unto righteousness, and with the mouth confession is made unto salvation. For the Scripture says, 'Whoever believes on Him will not be put to shame.'"
– Romans 10: 9-11 (NKJV)

"God decided in advance to adopt us into his own family by bringing us to himself through Jesus Christ. This is what he wanted to do, and it gave him great pleasure." – Ephesians 1:5 (NLT)

"Therefore if you have any encouragement from being united with Christ, if any comfort from his love, if any common sharing in the Spirit, if any tenderness and compassion, then make my joy complete by being like-minded, having the same love, being one in spirit and of one mind." – Philippians 2: 1-2 (NIV)

DEVOTION

We are coming to the end of this set of devotions and (in the churchiest voice you can imagine) I would be remiss if I didn't offer you a relationship with Jesus Christ. You can do all of the devotions in the world; you can attend every church service and bible study; you can listen to all of the worship music available. However, none of that means a thing if you do not have a personal relationship with God. God already knows about your situation. God knows about your faults and knows about your gifts. God desires to be with you. While you were still in sin, Jesus died for you! Yes, you! All you have to do is say "Yes" and allow God to transform your life. I encourage you to accept

Jesus as your Lord and Savior. If you've already done so, recommit yourself today. Don't let another second go by. Submitting to Jesus with my whole heart is the best decision I have ever made and there is plenty of salvation for you too! Choose God today!

PRAYER

Lord, I say yes to your will and I say yes to your way. Lord, I don't want to be a Christian by my words but by my actions. I believe that you died for me and rose with all power in your hands. Because you died for me, I will honor you with my whole heart, my mind, and everything that is within me. I am not perfect, but I desire to do better. I surrender myself to you. I say "yes" to you. I accept you as my personal Savior. In the name of Jesus I pray. Amen.

NOTES

_____
_____
_____
_____
_____
_____
_____
_____
_____
_____
_____
_____
_____

DAY 28
Rest In The Presence Of God

"He says, 'Be still, and know that I am God; I will be exalted among the nations, I will be exalted in the earth.'"
– Psalm 46:10 (NIV)

"You will keep in perfect peace those whose minds are steadfast, because they trust in you." – Isaiah 26:3 (NIV)

"Come to me, all you who are weary and burdened, and I will give you rest. Take my yoke upon you and learn from me, for I am gentle and humble in heart, and you will find rest for your souls. For my yoke is easy and my burden is light." – Matthew 11:28-30 (NIV)

Do not be anxious about anything, but in every situation, by prayer and petition, with thanksgiving, present your requests to God. And the peace of God, which transcends all understanding, will guard your hearts and minds in Christ Jesus. – Philippians 4:6-7 (NIV)

DEVOTION

At times you have to be by yourself and spend time with the Lord. Today I encourage you to spend at least twenty minutes alone with God. You won't find a prompted prayer, but I have included a list of songs that you can listen to while you meditate. Talk to God about whatever you like. There are lines on the next page if you like to journal. I hope you find rest for your soul.

SONGS

Heart of Worship – Michael W. Smith   Indescribable – Kierra Sheard
So Will I (100 Billion X) – Hillsong Worship

JOURNAL ENTRY:

Dear God,

DAY 29
An Everyday Choice

> *"But if serving the LORD seems undesirable to you, then choose for yourselves this day whom you will serve, whether the gods your ancestors served beyond the Euphrates, or the gods of the Amorites, in whose land you are living. But as for me and my household, we will serve the LORD." – Joshua 24:15 (NIV)*

DEVOTION

Many times we talk about choosing the Lord as if it is one large decision that we make once in a lifetime. Many people believe that when you choose Jesus as your Lord and Savior, you are set for life. While scriptures do tell us that all who call on the Lord will be saved, I would like to challenge you to consider every decision we make as an opportunity to choose the Lord. Every day you wake up, you must choose to serve the Lord rather than your own desires. Several internet sources say that we make over 35,000 choices a day. Do we speed or do we follow the speed limit? Do we get up immediately or do we press the snooze button? Do we go to Bible study or do we go home because we are tired? Do we argue with our neighbor or do we turn the other cheek? There are thousands of choices we make each day. Do you ever choose the Lord? Even with the small choices, do you consider how God may be glorified? Choose for yourselves this day, this hour, this minute, this second. Whom will you serve?

PRAYER

Lord, change my heart and my mind so that I may honor you with all of my choices. Remind me that I was created to bring you glory. My sole purpose centers on glorifying you. For this reason, every choice I make should be rooted in your will. I repent for every time I have chosen my own desires without considering how my witness may be impacted. I choose you. I choose your plan. I choose your will. In the name of Jesus I pray, Amen.

NOTES

DAY 30
Pressing Forward

"Therefore, my dear friends, as you have always obeyed--not only in my presence, but now much more in my absence – continue to work out your salvation with fear and trembling, for it is God who works in you to will and to act in order to fulfill his good purpose. Do everything without grumbling or arguing, so that you may become blameless and pure, "children of God without fault in a warped and crooked generation." Then you will shine among them like stars in the sky as you hold firmly to the word of life. And then I will be able to boast on the day of Christ that I did not run or labor in vain." – Philippians 2:12-16 (NIV)

Not that I have already obtained all this, or have already arrived at my goal, but I press on to take hold of that for which Christ Jesus took hold of me. Brothers and sisters, I do not consider myself yet to have taken hold of it. But one thing I do: Forgetting what is behind and straining toward what is ahead, I press on toward the goal to win the prize for which God has called me heavenward in Christ Jesus. – Philippians 3:12-14 (NIV)

DEVOTION

You have made it to the end of this set of devotions, but I hope this is not the end of your journey to get closer to God. I hope that through these devotions, you have grown; you have been delivered; you have been renewed; and you have committed or recommitted to Christ. However, this is only the beginning. You have a purpose in this life, and I pray that you receive the wisdom and strength to fulfil it. Keep moving forward. Leave the past in the past. Finish the race. Finish strong.

PRAYER

Lord, as these devotions come to an end, teach me how to continue this practice of devoting time to you. Show me how to shake off bad habits and show me positive habits to continue. Teach me how to endure until my race on earth is finished. Lord, continue to take everything out of me that is not like you. Fill me with your Holy Spirit. Teach me how to walk in your will and in your way. Teach me to seek after you every day of my life. In the name of Jesus I pray. Amen.

NOTES

Conclusion

I am delighted that you made it to the end of this set of devotions! Read this over and over again as needed. Hopefully you gained something that will aid you in your journey. I am on the same path, working out my salvation just like you. Everyday isn't easy, but God is faithful. I am so happy that I was, and continue to be, obedient to God. I have grown so much and am so excited about what the future holds. I am here for you if you ever want to talk. I will pray with you. I will pray for you. I will give the best advice I can.

And now, as you move forward I pray that you will do as the Apostle Paul instructed the church at Collasae in Colossians 1:10-14, "…*walk in a manner worthy of the Lord, fully pleasing to him, bearing fruit in every good work and increasing in the knowledge of God. [May you be] strengthened with all power, according to his glorious might, for all endurance and patience with joy, giving thanks to the Father, who has qualified you to share in the inheritance of the saints in light. He has delivered us from the domain of darkness and transferred us to the kingdom of his beloved Son, in whom we have redemption, the forgiveness or sins.*" (NIV)

Thanks for reading and God's blessings on you future!

Yours in Christ,

Erica R. Bluford
TheTrueLifetimeCommitment@gmail.com

ERICA R BLUFORD

THE TRUE
LIFETIME
COMMITMENT

www.ingramcontent.com/pod-product-compliance
Lightning Source LLC
Chambersburg PA
CBHW032135090426
42743CB00007B/603